Tales of The Great Female Muslim Sufi Saint from Basra

by

Muhammad Vandestra

2018

Content

Prolog---7

Rabia Al-Adawiyya The Female Muslim Sufi Saint from Basra---11

The Poem of Rabia Al-Basri---19

Author Bio--23

Prolog

Running with fire in one hand and water in the other, Rabia explained, "I am going to burn paradise and douse hellfire so that both veils may be lifted from those on the quest, and they will become sincere of purpose. God's servants will learn to see Him without hope for reward or fear of punishment. As it is now, if you took away hope for reward or fear of punishment, no one would obey."

This was the mentality of the most famous female Sufi saint, Rabia al-Adawiyya, who set forth the doctrine of Divine Love. She maintained praises of God weren't meant to be merely performed with the tongue, ears, eyes, hands, or feet — but with the wakeful heart.

"O Sons of Adam, from the eye, there is no way-station to the Real. From the tongue, there is no path to Him. Hearing is the highway of complainers. Hand and foot dwell in perplexity. The matter falls to the heart. Strive for a wakeful heart." (Rabia al-Adawiyya)

Born in year 717 to a poor family in Basra, Rabia al-Adawiyya, was the fourth daughter to her parents. She later became an orphan and was sold into slavery. According to Farid ad-Din Attar, Rabia ran away from her owner and put her face to the ground saying, "All I want is for You to be pleased with me, to know whether You are pleased with me or not." She heard a reply reassuring her not to be sad and promising her good. Rabia then went back to her owner.

One night, while she prostrated in prayer to God, her owner overheard her and witnessed a chain-less lantern suspended above her head light up the entire room. Upon this sight, the owner freed Rabi'a, and she spent her life in devotion to God.

According to Attar's "Memorial of the Friends of God," which holds the most thorough account of Rabia life, Rabia of Basra is considered one of the Sufi masters. Ironically, during her time, people referred to the masters as the "ranks of men." However, the deep Sufi concept of God's Unity leaves no room for individuals, gender, or status.

Rabia sincerity and love resulted in her being accredited by the men of her time. She delivered passionate and eye-opening words of wisdom to them regarding God, and they took her teachings to heart.

Salih Murri, God's mercy upon him, often used to say, "Whoever knocks at a door will have it opened in the end."

Once Rabi'a was present. She said, "How long will you say, 'He will open it again?' When did He close it that He will open it again?"

Salih said, "Amazing! An ignorant man and a wise, weak woman."

She referred to herself as a "weak woman," and so others called her this as well. However, her title was contrary to her actions, as she was a strong-willed woman who criticized and helped develop the other Sufi masters of her time.

Rabia lived the life of an ascetic, for her only concern was God. She paved the way for later female saints, and she reached a state which all Sufis strive for through the destruction of her nafs (ego/self). She developed a relationship with God built on love and tawakkul (trust). She didn't devote herself to Him out of desires for reward or fear of burning; rather, she only wanted to please God and never be cut off.

'Attār references Rabi'a al-Adawiyya in his famous "The Conference of the Birds" mystical poem:

"No, she wasn't a single woman,

But a hundred men over:

Robed in the quintessence of pain

From foot to face, immersed in the Truth,

Effaced in the radiance of God,

And liberated from all superfluous excess."

Rabia Al-Adawiyya The Female Muslim Sufi Saint from Basra

Rabia, the daughter of Ismail, a woman celebrated for her holy life, and a native of Basra, belonged to the tribe of Adi. Al Qushairi says in his treatise on Sufism, "She used to say when holding converse with God, 'Consume with fire O God, a presumptuous heart which loveth Thee.' On one of these occasions a voice spoke to her and said, 'That we shall not do. Think not of us an ill thought.' Often in the silence of the night she would go on the roof of her house and say, 'The lover is now with his beloved, but I rejoice in being alone with Thee.'"

When Rabia grew up her father and mother died. At that time there was a famine in Basra. She came into the possession of an evil man, who sold her as a slave. The master who bought her treated her hardly, and exacted all kinds of menial services from her. One day, when she was seeking to avoid the rude gaze of a stranger, she slipped on the path and fell, breaking her wrist. Lying there with her face to the ground, she said "Lord, I am far from my own, a captive and an orphan, and my wrist has just been broken, and yet none of these things grieve me. Only this one thought causes me disquiet; it is that I know not if Thou art satisfied with me." She then heard a voice, "Vex not thyself, O Rabia, for at the day of Resurrection We shall give thee such a rank that the angels nearest Us shall envy thee." Rabia went home with her heart at peace.

One night, Rabia's master being awake, heard the sound of her voice. He perceived Rabia with her head bent, saying, "My Lord, Thou knowest that the desire of my heart is to seek Thy approbation, and that its only wish is to obey Thy commands. If I had liberty of action, I would not remain a single instant without doing Thee service; but Thou hast delivered me into the hands of a creature, and therefore I am hindered in the same." Her master said to himself that it was not possible any longer to treat her as a slave, and as soon as daybreak appeared, he said to her, "O Rabia, I make thee free. If thou desirest, remain here, and we shall be at thy service. If thou dost not wish to to stay here, go whithersoever it pleaseth thee."

Then Rabia departed from them and devoted herself entirely to works of piety. One day when she was making the pilgrimage to the Kaaba she halted in the desert and exclaimed, "My God, my heart is a prey to perplexity in the midst of this solitude. I am a stone, and so is the Kaaba; what can it do for me? That which I need is to contemplate Thy face." At these words a voice came from the Most High, "O Rabia, wilt thou bear alone that which the whole world cannot? When Moses desired to see Our Face we showed It to a mountain, which dissolved into a thousand fragments."

Abda, the servant maid of Rabia, relates as follows, "Rabia used to pass the whole night in prayer, and 30at morning dawn she took a light sleep in her oratory till daylight, and I have heard her say when she sprang in dread from her couch, 'O my soul, how long wilt thou sleep? Soon thou shalt sleep to rise no more, till the call shall summon thee on the day of resurrection.'"

Hasan Basri once asked Rabia if she ever thought of marrying. She answered, "The marriage contract can be entered into by those who have possession of their free-will. As for me, I have no will to dispose of; I belong to the Lord, and I rest in the shadow of His commandments, counting myself as nothing." "But," said Hasan, "how have you arrived at such a degree of piety?" "By annihilating myself completely."

Being asked on another occasion why she did not marry, she answered, "There are three things which cause me anxiety." "And what are they?" "One is to know whether at the moment of death I shall be able to take my faith with me intact. The second is whether in the Day of Resurrection the register of my actions will be placed in my right hand or not. The third is to know, when some are led to Paradise and some to hell, in which direction I shall be led." "But," they cried, "none of us know any of these things." "What!" she answered, "when I have such objects to pre-occupy my mind, should I think of a husband?"

Someone asked her one day, "Whence comest thou?" "From the other world," was her reply. "And whither goest thou?" "Into the other world." "And what doest thou in this world." "I jest with it by eating its bread and doing the works of the other world in it." "O Rabia," said another to her, "dost thou love the Lord?" "Truly," she replied, "I love Him." "And dost thou regard Satan as an enemy?" "I love the Lord so much," she answered, "that I do not trouble myself about the enmity of Satan."

One night she saw the Prophet (on whom be peace) in a dream. He saluted her and said, "Rabia, lovest thou me?" "O Prophet of God," she replied, "is there anyone who does not love thee? Yet the love of the Most High fills my heart to such a degree that there is no room for love or hatred towards anyone else."

On one occasion she was asked, "Dost thou see Him Whom thou servest?" "If I did not see Him," she said, "I would not serve Him." She was frequently found in tears, and, being asked the reason why, replied, "I fear that at the last moment a Voice may cry, 'Rabia is not worthy to appear in Our court.'" The following question was put to her, "If one of His servants truly repents, will the Lord accept it or not?" "As long as God does not grant repentance," she replied, "how can anyone repent? And if He does grant it, there is no doubt that he will accept it."

Once when Rabia had immured herself for a long while in her house without coming forth, her servant said to her, "Lady, come forth out of this house and contemplate the works of the Most High." "Nay," said Rabia, "enter rather into thyself and contemplate His work in thyself." Having kept a strict fast for seven days and nights in order to give herself to prayer, on the eighth night she seemed to hear her emaciated body say, "O Rabia, how long wilt thou torture me without mercy?" Whilst she was holding this soliloquy with herself, suddenly someone knocked at the door, and a man brought in some food in a bowl. Rabia took it and set it down; then while she went to light the lamp, a cat came and ate the food. No sooner had Rabia returned and seen what had happened than she said to herself, "I will break my fast on water." As she went to draw water her lamp went out. She then uttered a deep sigh, and said, "Lord, why dost thou make me wretched?" Whereupon she heard a voice saying, "O Rabia, if thou desirest it, I will give thee the whole world for thine own; but I shall have to take away the love which thou hast for Me from thy heart, for the love of Me and of the world cannot exist together." "Hearing myself thus addressed," said Rabia, "I entirely expelled from my heart the love of earthly things, and resolutely turned my gaze away from them. For thirty years I have not prayed without saying to myself, 'This prayer, perhaps, is the last which I shall pray,' and I have never been tired of saying, 'My God, let me be so absorbed in Thy love that no other affection may find room in my heart.'"

One day some men of learning and piety came to her and said, "The Most High has crowned His chosen saints with the gift of performing miracles, but such privileges have never been granted to a woman. How didst thou attain to such a high degree?" "What you say is true," she answered, "but, on the other hand, women have never been so infatuated with themselves as men, nor have they ever claimed divinity."

Hasan Basri relates, "One day when I had been to Rabia who had fallen sick, to ask after her, I saw seated at her gate a merchant who wept. 'Why are you weeping?' I asked him. 'I have just brought for Rabia,' he answered, 'this purse of gold, and I am troubled in mind, not knowing whether she will accept it or not. Go in Hasan, and ask whether she will.' Then I went in, and no sooner had I reported to her the words of this merchant than she said to me, 'Thou knowest well, O Hasan, that the Most High gives daily bread even to those who do not worship Him; how then will He not give it to those whose hearts are aglow with love to Him? Besides, ever since I have known God, I have turned my eyes away from all except Him. How can I accept anyone's money when I know not whether it has been gained by lawful or unlawful means? Present then my excuses to this merchant, and let him go.'"

Another merchant visiting Rabia found her house in ill repair. He presented her with a new house. Rabia had no sooner entered it than, seeing paintings on the wall, she became absorbed in contemplating them. Recovering herself, she quitted the house, and refused to re-enter it, saying, "I fear lest my heart may become attached to this house to such a degree that I neglect preparation for the other world."

One day Abdul Wahid and Sofiân Tsavri went to see Rabia in her illness. They were so touched by the sight of her weakness that for some moments they could not speak a word. At last Sofiân said, "O Rabia, pray that the Lord may lighten thy sufferings." "O Sofiân," she answered, "who has sent me these sufferings?" "The Most High," he said. "Very well," she replied, "if it is his will that this trial come upon me, how can I, ignoring His will, ask Him to remove it?" "Rabia," said Sofiân, "I am not capable of talking to thee about thy own affairs; talk to me about mine." "Well," answered Rabia, "if thou hadst not an inclination to this low world, thou wouldst be a man without fault." "Then," relates Sofiân, "I cried with tears, 'My God, canst Thou be satisfied with me?'" "O Sofiân," said Rabia, "dost thou not blush at saying to the Lord, 'Canst Thou be satisfied with me?' without having done a single thing to please him?"

Malik Dinar recounts the following: "I went to see Rabia, and found her drinking water out of a broken pitcher. She was lying stretched on an old mat, with a brick for her pillow. I was pierced to the heart at the sight, and said, "O Rabia, I have rich friends; if you will let me, I will go and ask them for something for you." "You have spoken ill, Malik," she replied; 'it is the Lord who, to them as to me, gives daily bread. He Who provides for the needs of the rich, shall He not provide for the necessities of the poor? If He wills that it should be thus with us, we shall gladly submit to His will.'"

On one occasion when Malik Dinar, Hasan Basri and Shaqiq were with her, the conversation turned on sincerity of heart towards God. Hasan Basri said, "He has not sincere love to God who does not bear with constancy the afflictions which the Lord sends him." "That remark savours of self-conceit," said Rabia. Shaqiq observed, "He is not sincere who does not render thanks for afflictions." "There is a higher degree of sincerity than that," said Rabia. Malik Dinar suggested, "He is not sincere who does not find delight in the afflictions which the Lord sends." "That is not the purest sincerity," she remarked. Then they asked her to define sincerity. She said, "He is not sincere who does not forget the pain of affliction through his absorption in God."

One of the learned theologians of Basra, once visiting Rabia, began to enlarge upon the defects of the world. "You must be very fond of the world," said Rabia, "for if you were not, you would not talk so much about it. He who really intends to buy something keeps on discussing it. If you were really disentangled from it, what would you care about its merits or its faults?"

Other sayings of Rabia were these, "My God, if on the day of judgment Thou sendest me to hell, I shall reveal a secret which will make hell fly far from me." "O Lord, give all Thou destinest for me of the goods of this world to Thy enemies, and all that Thou reservest for me in Paradise to Thy friends, for it is Thou only Whom I seek." "My God, if it is from fear of hell that I serve Thee, condemn me to burn in hell; and if it is for the hope of Paradise, forbid me entrance there; but if it is for Thy sake only, deny me not the sight of Thy face."

Rabia died a.d. 752, and was buried near Jerusalem. Her tomb was a centre of pilgrimage during the Middle Ages.

The Poem of Rabia Al-Basri

O God, Another Night is passing away

O God, Another Night is passing away,
Another Day is rising --
Tell me that I have spent the Night well so I can be at peace,
Or that I have wasted it, so I can mourn for what is lost.
I swear that ever since the first day You brought me back to life,
The day You became my Friend,
I have not slept --
And even if You drive me from your door,
I swear again that we will never be separated.
Because You are alive in my heart.

I carry a torch in one hand

I carry a torch in one hand
And a bucket of water in the other:
With these things I am going to set fire to Heaven
And put out the flames of Hell
So that voyagers to God can rip the veils
And see the real goal.

I have two ways of loving You:

I have two ways of loving You:
A selfish one
And another way that is worthy of You.
In my selfish love, I remember You and You alone.
In that other love, You lift the veil
And let me feast my eyes on Your Living Face.

Brothers, my peace is in my aloneness

Brothers, my peace is in my aloneness.
My Beloved is alone with me there, always.
I have found nothing in all the worlds
That could match His love,
This love that harrows the sands of my desert.
If I come to die of desire
And my Beloved is still not satisfied,
I would live in eternal despair.

To abandon all that He has fashioned
And hold in the palm of my hand
Certain proof that He loves me---
That is the name and the goal of my search.

O my Lord, if I worship you

O my Lord,

if I worship you
from fear of hell, burn me in hell.

If I worship you
from hope of Paradise, bar me from its gates.

But if I worship you
for yourself alone, grant me then the beauty of your
Face.

O my Lord, the stars glitter

O my Lord,
the stars glitter
and the eyes of men are closed.
Kings have locked their doors
and each lover is alone with his love.

Here, I am alone with you.

Author Biography

Muhammad Vandestra has been a columnist, health writer, soil scientist, magazine editor, web designer & kendo martial arts instructor. A writer by day and reader by night, he write fiction and non-fiction books for adult and children. He lives in West Jakarta City.

Muhammad Vandestra merupakan seorang kolumnis, editor majalah, perancang web & instruktur beladiri kendo. Seorang penulis pada siang hari dan pembaca di malam hari, Ia menulis buku fiksi dan non-fiksi untuk anak-anak dan dewasa. Sekarang ia tinggal dan menetap di Kota Jakarta Barat.

Blog **https://www.vandestra.blogspot.com**

Made in the USA
Middletown, DE
04 November 2021